As a Man Thinketh

21ST CENTURY EDITION

Other books available at
WWW.SUCCESSBOOKS.NET

The Way to Weath *by Benjamin Franklin*
The Richest Man in Babylon *by George S. Clason*
Think and Grow Rich *by Napoleon Hill*
A Message to Garcia *by Elbert Hubbard*
and many more

As a Man Thinketh

21st Century Edition

THE WISDOM OF

JAMES ALLEN

REPHRASED BY

CHARLES CONRAD

BEST SUCCESS BOOKS

www.SuccessBooks.net

CONTENTS

INTRODUCTION

WIDELY considered the greatest self-help book of all-time, *As a Man Thinketh* reveals how our thoughts determine our character, circumstances, health, appearance, and achievements. The choice is ours: either master our thoughts to create the life we want, or remain mired in frustration and failure.

James Allen (1864–1912) was born into a poor, working-class British family. When he was fifteen, James's father was tragically killed, and he dropped out of school to work and support his family. He was a young laborer during the harsh early years of the Industrial Revolution.

For the next twenty years, James pulled himself up through the factory system. Reading voraciously and developing his writing skills during his few spare hours, he eventually reached the level of an executive's assistant.

Through it all, James focused his thoughts on truth, beauty, virtue, and success. These qualities came to define his life.

At age 38, James retired from business to become a writer and contemplative philosopher. He moved to a small cottage in the country with his beloved wife, Lily. Together, they edited a philosophical journal, *The Epoch*, and James poured out his thoughts in a steady stream of books.

After his death, Lily continued to edit *The Epoch* and publish James's posthumous works, ensuring that his legacy would endure. Today, James Allen's books are read more widely than ever, inspiring millions around the globe.

While James's writing was exceptionally clear for its time, *As a Man Thinketh*—like any 100-year-old book—uses archaic language that can be difficult to grasp. For this 21st Century Edition, I have rephrased James's ideas in contemporary English, making his wisdom available to today's readers.

—CHARLES CONRAD

FOREWORD

Mind is the master power that molds and makes;
We are mind, in one of the guises it takes.

Taking the tool of thought, we sculpt what we will,
Shaping our lives for good or ill.

We think in secret, and it comes to pass;
The world is our reflection — the mind's looking-glass.

THIS handbook is the result of meditation and experience. It is not a theoretical treatise, but a practical guide. Its aim is to inspire men and women to realize that "we are the makers of ourselves" by virtue of the thoughts we choose and encourage.

Mind is the great weaver of our lives, shaping both our inner character and outer circumstances. Up till now, you may have woven in ignorance and pain; but from this day forth, you can weave in enlightenment and happiness.

—JAMES ALLEN

CHAPTER I

Thought Shapes Character

T HE proverb, "As a man thinks in his heart, so is he," encompasses our character, our condition, and the circumstances of our lives. We literally *are our thoughts.*

What is our character, but the sum total of our thoughts over time?

As a plant grows from a seed, so our every act grows from a seed of thought. Everything we do or say begins in our minds. Even when our actions *seem* spontaneous or unpremeditated, they are driven by thoughts.

Behavior is the blossom of thought, and joy and suffering are its fruits. We reap the harvest—sweet or bitter—of our inner garden.

Thoughts in the mind determine your course,
Steering your life for better or worse.

If you dwell on thoughts that are petty and unkind,
Pain will follow you as the ox's plough—behind.

If you dwell on thoughts that are noble and pure,
Joy will follow you as your own shadow—sure.

The law of cause and effect is as valid in the invisible realm of thought as it is in the visible, material world. A noble character doesn't appear by chance; it is the natural result of consistent, right thinking—the cumulative effect of dwelling on noble thoughts.

We are built up or brought down by ourselves. In the mind, we can build a fortress of joy, strength, and peace; or we can forge the weapons of thought that will bring about our own destruction. By right thinking, we harmonize with the divine intelligence of the universe; by wrong thinking, we descend to the level of beasts. We choose the direction along which our character develops, and this determines the course of our life.

Of all the uplifting, ennobling thoughts we can dwell upon, none is more powerful than this: that we are the masters of our own thoughts, the authors of our own characters, and thus the makers of our own destinies.

With the powers of intelligence and love, we hold the key to turn every situation to our advantage. We have the ability to transform ourselves and our circumstances.

You are the master of your fate. Today, you may be mired in failure and misery because of past mistakes rooted in foolish thinking. But if you grasp this new understanding of the power of thought, you can begin to direct your energies in a positive direction. By taking conscious control of your mind, you can rejuvenate your life.

You don't have to take this on faith. Try it. Watch, control, and change your thoughts, and observe the results. It's not a matter of blind belief but of investigation, consistent practice, and experience. Begin with the most trivial, everyday concerns—even the simplest subjects are portals to self-knowledge.

Diamonds are obtained by mining under the earth. Dig deep within your soul, and you will gain new riches of understanding, wisdom, and power. You will realize the truth of the statement, "Seek and you will find; knock and the door will be opened."

CHAPTER 2

Thought Shapes Circumstance

THE mind is like a garden which can be cultivated or allowed to run wild. Either way, it will bring forth results. If seeds of intelligent thought are planted and nurtured, they will grow into a healthful harvest. If the garden is left to chance, weed-seeds will blow in, take root, and flourish, producing nothing of use.

Just as a gardener weeds, waters, and cares for their plot, we must cultivate our mind—weeding out negative, mistaken, useless thoughts, while encouraging positive, true, fruitful thoughts. Even good seeds, not continually cared for, will be crowded out by weeds.

Character is simply the sum of our thoughts. And character manifests itself in our environment and through our circumstances. So, the outer condition of our life is always a reflection of our inner state.

This doesn't mean that we have brought about *everything* in our life at a given moment (other people have their creative powers, too, which may cooperate or conflict with ours), or that we have earned every circumstance that comes our way. But our thoughts are so closely tied to our circumstances, they are inseparable. Even when events or situations are out of our control, our thoughts, reactions, and responses are still within our control.

As a general rule, though, we are responsible for where we are. *Who we are* has brought us here. This is true of those who are happy in their surroundings, and equally true of those who feel out of harmony with theirs.

The universe, and everything in it, is progressive and evolving. Wherever we find ourselves, we are here so that we can *grow*. Once we learn the lesson of a given circumstance, it passes away, and new circumstances arise.

We are victims of circumstance as long as we consider ourselves pawns of fate, tossed here and there by outside forces. But if you realize your creative power—if you assume responsibility for the seeds and soil of your inner garden—then you become the master of your own destiny.

The soul attracts whatever it secretly holds—that which it loves, and that which it fears. It rises to the height of its highest ideals; it falls to the level of its basest desires. The soul broadcasts its frequency, and circumstance returns it.

Every thought-seed sown in the mind—or allowed to fall there and take root—blossoms into action, bears the fruit of circumstance, and produces more of its own kind. Good thoughts bear good fruit; bad thoughts, bad fruit.

The outer world springs from the inner world. Everything external to us—good or bad, desirable or undesirable—should be used for our education and benefit. We can learn from both pleasure and pain, happiness and misery, success and failure.

No one ends up in jail by an accident of fate (unless they are falsely convicted). When a person entertains degraded, dishonest, violent thoughts, they start down a pathway that leads inexorably to crime. Circumstances do not force honest people to turn to crime. Circumstances only provide an *opportunity* for criminal thoughts, previously nurtured in secret, to blossom into action.

Circumstances don't shape us, so much as they *reveal* us. As the masters of our thoughts, we are the authors of our environments. As the sole gardener of your own mind, you have more power than any other force in shaping your environment and your destiny.

People do not attract what they want, but what they *are*. Our whims and daydreams may not come true, but *who we are* will always be manifest in our external lives. The content of our minds and hearts cannot remain hidden for long. Fate is not something outside you, utterly beyond your control. You *are* your fate. Character is destiny.

Your wishes and dreams will only come true when they are in harmony with your thoughts and actions. It's futile to fight against circumstances. You cannot change your surroundings while continuing to think the same thoughts that brought you here. To improve your circumstances, improve yourself. Self-discipline is key to obtaining anything you want, no matter whether your aims are high or low. Even those who simply desire wealth must make many personal sacrifices to earn it. Think of how many more sacrifices it takes to develop a resilient, trustworthy, inspiring, fully-rounded character.

We may have worthy goals, but our efforts will be thwarted if our thoughts are not in alignment with them. Picture a young man born into poverty who rightly wishes for money, but takes a shortcut to get it—by stealing from his employer. He is only digging himself a deeper hole.

Picture a woman who suffers from debilitating health problems because of her diet of processed foods and sugary drinks. She wishes to be healthy and is willing to visit doctors and take prescription drugs, but she refuses to change her lifestyle. She can never gain a healthy body without a healthy mindset.

Picture an employer who pays their workers the bare minimum, and refuses them health insurance, paid vacation time, and other benefits. They wish for profits, but lasting success cannot be built on the backs of discontented, disloyal, overworked, underproductive employees.

It is not enough just to have a positive goal. As the three examples above show, our goals must be in harmony with our thoughts—both conscious and unconscious—or they will never be realized.

The interplay between thought and circumstance is too complex to judge a person's heart and mind simply based on their current circumstances. One entrepreneur may be upright and honest in certain aspects, yet their business fails. Another may be boastful and dishonest in certain aspects, yet their business succeeds. It's common to say that the first entrepreneur failed *because* they are honest, while the second succeeded *because* they are dishonest—but this is a mistaken conclusion. It assumes that some people are completely virtuous while others are completely evil, which is a simplification. Upon closer examination, the more dishonest entrepreneur may possess some virtues—like decisiveness and efficiency—that the more honest entrepreneur lacks.

It soothes our vanity to say that we failed because we were too good, or that we're broke because we're too honest. But this isn't true. Until you have wiped every impure thought from your mind and cleansed every spot from your soul, how can you know that your sufferings are the result of your virtues and not your faults? Or that victory will not come you tomorrow, if you persist through today's setback?

The purpose of suffering is to to teach, strengthen, and purify. Do not whine and pity yourself; learn and grow from your faults and failures. Search for the hidden justice that rules your life. Instead of kicking against circumstances, use them as stair-steps to greater heights, as means of discovering new powers within yourself.

Law, not confusion, rules the universe. Justice, not injustice, is its guiding principle. *You attract what you are. You get what you give.*

Thistle seeds can't yield corn, and corn seeds can't yield thistles. Good thoughts can't produce bad results, and bad thoughts can't produce good results. Everyone understands this law in the natural world, but few understand it in the mental and moral world.

A blessed life is the sure result of right thought. By *blessedness*, I don't mean mere material wealth—a person can be rich and miserable, after all. Blessedness is a state of harmony and happiness. This is the measure of the good life.

You cannot directly choose your circumstances; but by changing your thoughts, you can indirectly reshape your circumstances. As you change your attitude towards things and other people, they will change towards you. The world will soften towards you; people will be eager to help you. New opportunities will spring up at every turn.

The world is your kaleidoscope; the ever-changing combinations of colors it presents to you are exquisitely tuned to reflect the hues of your ever-moving thoughts.

You will be what you will to be.
Only failure seeks contentment
In that alibi, "environment."
The mind scorns it and is free.

It masters time, it conquers space,
It outwits that trickster, Chance;
It takes the crown from Circumstance,
And puts it in a servant's place.

The human will, that unseen force,
Offspring of mind and soul,
Can forge a path to any goal,
And conquer anything in its course.

CHAPTER 3

Thought Shapes
Health & Appearance

THE body is the servant of the mind. It obeys the mind's commands, whether conscious or unconscious. Our conscious mind chooses to contract muscles and move our bodies; while our unconscious mind directs the autonomic nervous system, regulating our heartbeat, circulation, breathing, and other bodily processes.

Our health and appearance, like our circumstances, are shaped by our thoughts. Negative thoughts direct the body to disorder, disease, and decline. Uplifting thoughts energize the body and impart a youthful glow.

Over time, unhealthful thoughts express themselves in a weak, overweight, or sickly body. Slothful thoughts encourage a sedentary lifestyle. Both self-indulgent and self-loathing thoughts can cause overeating. Anxious, stressful, and fearful thoughts set off our internal alarm system—blood pressure rises, breathing becomes fast and shallow, and the body releases stress-response hormones. When this is repeated frequently, our glands are depleted and our immune system weakened.

The opposite is also true—positive thoughts boost our health and immunity. Strong, confident, caring, grateful, happy thoughts express themselves in a vigorous, vibrant, graceful, beautiful body.

While you may inherit a genetic blueprint from your parents, the tools for building your body are in your hands, and the materials that will be used are up to you. (These include the foods you eat and the exercises you perform.) Two builders, working from the same blueprint, can produce two entirely different houses—one cheap, sloppy, soon-dilapidated; the other fine-crafted, stately, and enduring.

Diet and exercise actually begin in the mind. What will you eat? How will you move your body? Your dominant thoughts determine the answers. A person who reads about nutrition and often thinks about which foods are the most nourishing will naturally make healthy choices, without strain or self-deprivation. A person who focuses their mind on athletics or muscular development, combining enthusiasm and dedication with a sound training program, will surely build a strong and speedy physique. And in athletic competitions, intelligent planning, quick thinking, and mental determination lead to victory.

Healthy thoughts become healthy habits. Hold a vision of yourself aglow with energy and vitality, act in harmony with that vision, and you will grow to embody it.

If you wish to protect your body from sickness, purify your mind. If you wish to be physically attractive, beautify your mind. Thoughts of jealousy, hatred, indifference, disappointment, and despair rob the body of its natural radiance. A "sour face" is the expression of sour thoughts.

I know a 96-year-old woman with the bright, innocent face of a girl. And I know a 36-year-old man with a permanent frown, who looks at least twice his age. One is the outflowing of a sunny, friendly disposition; the other of discontent and a bad temper.

As you cannot have a light-filled, airy home unless you pull back the curtains and open the windows, you cannot have bright, happy countenance without opening your mind and letting in thoughts of joy, goodwill, and peace.

Those who remain pure in their thoughts grow old gracefully and serenely. Their waning years are bathed in beautiful, mellow hues, like a sunset over the ocean. I recently sat at the deathbed of a wise philosopher. He was not old except in years, and he died as sweetly and peacefully as he lived.

There is no better medicine than cheerful thought for curing and preventing bodily ills. To wish the best for all people; to find the good in everything; to be content in all circumstances—such thoughts are the portal to heaven.

CHAPTER 4

The Power of Purpose

I N order to accomplish anything, thought needs *purpose*. Too often, we allow our thoughts to drift aimlessly on the seas of life; purpose powers them to a desired destination.

Those who lack a central purpose in life fall prey to worries, fears, and petty troubles, and end up stuck in self-pity. They may appear virtuous, because they lack any glaring faults and make no great mistakes, but they take a long, winding route to failure and unhappiness just the same.

Conceive a central purpose for your life and set out to accomplish it. It may be a noble ideal, such as spreading justice and freedom, or a worldly attainment, such as founding a successful corporation. Whatever it is, make it the focal point of your thoughts. Dedicate yourself to its realization. Thought becomes powerful as it is focused and concentrated.

As a person strives and fails, again and again, in the service of a worthy goal, their character is strengthened and deepened. They turn obstacles into stepping-stones. This is the measure of true success.

What if you are a student, are waiting for inspiration, or don't yet have a central purpose in mind? Start by focusing on the task at hand, whatever duty is before you at work, school, or home. Concentrate on doing your job as well as you can, even if it seems insignificant. This will develop and expand your ability to take on greater goals in the future.

You may have little or no experience, but—now that you know mental power can be developed by effort and exercise—you can begin to exert yourself. With patience and practice, you will grow exponentially stronger.

To begin to think with a purpose in mind, laying aside distractions and daydreams, is to enter the ranks of the successful—those who learn from their failures, find the advantage in every circumstance, think strongly, dare fearlessly, and act masterfully.

Once you conceive a purpose, create a plan for its attainment. Look neither to the right nor left—fears and doubts will only pull you off-track. Entertaining fear and doubt never accomplished anything. The power to *do* springs from the confidence that you *can*.

Allied with purpose, your every thought is energized, giving you the courage to face and overcome any obstacle. Purpose-driven thought is a creative force. Understand this, and you are ready to become something more than a bundle of jumbled thoughts and shifting sensations. Put it into practice, and you will become the master of your mental powers.

CHAPTER 5

The Path to Success

As you think, so you are.
As you are, so you act.
As you act, so you attain.

ALL that we achieve, or fail to achieve, is the result of our own thoughts. Your strengths and weaknesses, your virtues and faults, are entirely your own—they are not forced upon you by others or by circumstance. Only you can improve yourself.

Your happiness and suffering come from within. Only you can change your state. As you think, you are. As continue to think, you will be.

A strong person cannot help a weak person unless they *want* to be helped; even then, the weak person must work to become stronger. By your own efforts, you must develop in yourself the qualities you admire in another.

Throughout history, it has been common to think and say, "The many are oppressed because the few lord over them. Let us hate the leaders."

What if we reversed the perspective? "Good leaders are scarce because the majority of people are followers. Let's stop thinking and acting like helpless victims, rise up, and become leaders."

When a person realizes that their thoughts determine their experience of life, they have no desire to oppress others, nor can they be oppressed. They understand that the oppressor and the oppressed are cooperators in ignorance. They have compassion for all. They are free.

The only way to rise is to elevate your thoughts.

To achieve anything—even material possessions—we must lift our thoughts above sloth and self-indulgence. Successful people put off gratification, conceive goals, create plans, and execute those plans. They act independently, on their own initiative. They master their thoughts, and so master their circumstances.

The higher you elevate your thoughts—from your own good, to the good of your family and friends, to the good of all people, to the good of the whole earth and all creatures—the greater will be your success, and the more enduring your achievements.

Although it may seem so at times, the universe does *not* favor the greedy, the dishonest, and the violent. In fact, all forces—seen and unseen—rush to help the humble, the honest, and the generous. Teachers and prophets of all times and places have praised the same virtues, because they are written into the fabric of our nature. All spiritual and intellectual achievements come from contemplating the beautiful, the good, and the true.

Yes, some successful businessmen, artists, and scientists have been touched by pride and selfishness—but their accomplishments flowed from their virtues, not their vices. If they had rooted out all selfishness and been even more generous, their accomplishments would have been all the greater.

Those who give little accomplish little; those who give much accomplish much; those who give the most become the greatest.

All achievements—whether in business, science, the arts, or in personal development and spiritual evolution—are the result of purpose-driven thought. Goals differ, but the way to attain them is the same.

CHAPTER 6

Visions and Ideals

DREAMERS are the redeemers of the world. Humankind is blessed in good times, and sustained through hard times, by the visions of its dreamers. Inspired by their ideals, we work tirelessly to build a peaceful, just, compassionate society.

Composer, sculptor, painter, poet, prophet, sage—these are the artists of our ideals, the architects of heaven. The world is a better place because they lived.

The person who cherishes a beautiful vision in their heart will one day realize it. Explorers cherished visions of new worlds, and sailed the oceans to find them. Scientists cherished visions of tiny molecules and vast galaxies, and invented microscopes and telescopes to reveal them. Prophets cherished visions of a divine power permeating the universe, and entered into harmony with it.

Cherish your visions and ideals; cherish the music that moves your heart. For out of your love will flow your purpose, your unique contribution to better this world.

Aim high and dream big; for as you dream, you will become. Your life will expand to fill the contours of your vision.

As the towering oak was once an acorn, the greatest achievement was once an idea. Dreams are the seeds of reality.

Your circumstances may be unfavorable now, but they won't remain so for long if you conceive an ideal and strive for it. An interior transformation will soon express itself outwardly.

Picture a youth hard-pressed by poverty, confined for long hours in a stuffy workshop, unschooled and lacking all the arts of refinement. But he dreams of better things. He values intelligence, grace, and beauty. In his mind, he envisions his ideal life. He springs into action, using all his spare time and money—little as it is—to develop himself and expand his horizons. Soon, the workshop cannot hold him. His mind has so outgrown his surroundings that he casts them off like an old coat.

Years later, we see him as a grown man. He is the master of his mind, with which he exerts power and influence. He shoulders great responsibilities and creates products and services that benefit his customers. He inspires others to follow his example and improve their own lives. He has become one with his vision.

I have known men and women like this.

You, too, will realize the vision of your heart, be it beautiful, ugly, or a mixture of both. This is because you naturally gravitate towards that which you cherish most of all. You will rise as high as your greatest aspiration, or fall as low as your controlling desire.

The ignorant, seeing only the outward results and not the internal processes behind them, chalk up everything to chance and fate. Seeing a wealthy person, they say, "If only I were that lucky"; seeing a scientist, they say, "If only I were were born with brains"; seeing a beloved humanitarian, they say, "If only God had a purpose for me." They don't see the forming and holding of a vision, the years of training, and the overcoming of obstacles along the way. They don't see the struggles; they only see the success.

In all human endeavors there are efforts, and there are results. The result is proportional to the strength of effort. Chance or fate has nothing to do with it, except to the degree that we create our own luck and act on opportunities. Achievements are dreams realized.

The vision that you hold in your mind, the ideal that you cherish in your heart—this you will build your life by, and this you will become.

CHAPTER 7

Serenity

P EACE of mind is the crowning jewel of wisdom. It is the result of long, patient practice leading to the mastery of thoughts and moods. It indicates profound knowledge of the laws of nature and the mind.

A person can be calm in all circumstances only if they understand how their thoughts shape and color their experience, and have the mental agility to see things from new perspectives. Where others would say "all is lost," they remain steadfast, knowing they have the tools to turn any adversity into opportunity. They do not fear the unknown, for they trust in the law of cause and effect that governs the universe. They are resilient, and know how to adapt to change.

Even the average person, taking their first steps in tranquility, will benefit. In business and all other relationships, people prefer a calm, even-keeled partner. The more peaceful a person becomes, the greater their success and influence. Others will trust them, be drawn to them, and lean on them in times of trouble.

This poise—serenity—is the blossom of right thinking, the fruit of the soul. It is more desirable than gold. Mere wealth, without peace of mind, gives no satisfaction.

Think of how many people spoil their lives by stewing in thoughts of ingratitude, injustice, jealousy, anger, and rage. They carry conflict with them wherever they go.

What a joy it is to meet a person who exudes serenity. They stand strong and firm as a deeply-rooted, shade-giving tree. Through all kinds of weather, they comfort, encourage, and inspire all who come into their presence. The winds and storms of life cannot topple them.

Tempest-tossed souls, wherever you are, whatever your current circumstances, know this: In the ocean of life, there are isles of blessedness. The sunny shore of your ideal vision awaits you. Keep your hand firmly on the helm of thought. All that you need is within yourself—awaken your powers. Self-discipline is strength. Right thought is mastery. Calmness is power.

Say to your heart, "Peace, be still."